And Now This

And Now This

Poems by Terry Persun

MoonPath Press

Copyright © 2013 Terry Persun
all rights reserved

Poetry
ISBN 978-1-936657-05-6

Cover photo by Dorothy M. Persun
Author photo by Nicole J. Persun

Design by Tonya Namura
using Linux Libertine

MoonPath Press is dedicated to publishing the
best poets of the U.S. Northwest Pacific states

MoonPath Press
PO Box 1808
Kingston, WA 98346

MoonPathPress@yahoo.com

http://MoonPathPress.com

Acknowledgments

I am grateful to the editors of the following magazines in which these poems first appeared (sometimes in a different version): "In the Story," *Nightsun*; "Food Line," *The New Press*; "Shooting Puppies," *Yarrow*; "Saving Lives," *Impetus*; "The Dried Run," *Colorado-North Review*; "The Big Rock," *Whispers*; "The Black Man," *Howling Dog*; "Bottle Cap," *Hiram Poetry Review*; and "Cheating the Deer" and "Under the Surface," *Parting Gifts*.

I would also like to thank the editors of my previously published chapbooks and collections where some of these poems previously appeared (often with a different version of the poem). Those volumes include: *In the Story, Every Leaf, Three Lives, Barn Tarot, Hollow Goodbyes*, and *Plant-Animal-I*.

Lastly, but most importantly, I wish to thank Lana Hechtman Ayers for her close editorial attention to the content, selection, and organization of these poems.

Contents

I
First Memory, 5
In the Story of My Father, 6
War, 8
Cheating the Deer, 9
Food Line, 10
Kickball, 11
Shooting Puppies, 13
Saving Lives, 14
The Dried Run, 15
Wife Abuse, 16
The Big Rock, 18
Home, 19
Pointing the Barrel, 20
The Black Man, 21
Hay Ride, 23
The Tree House, 24
Headless, 25
Beyond Death, 26
Return to the Earth, 27
The Butternut Tree, 28

II
Dad, 31
Bottle Cap, 32
Conversation, 33
The Back Roads, 34
Fly Home, 35
And Now This, 36
Fed, 37
Friend, 38
Progress, 39
Under the Surface, 40

The Stock Barn Fire, 41
Cemetery Dance, 42
The Blank Slate, 43
Mourning, 44
Love Poem, 45
Notes, 46
Writing Poetry, 47
My Sister's Heart Attack, 48
The Question Never Asked, 49
Staring into the Past, 50
On Leaving, 51

About the Author, 53

And Now This

I

First Memory

I'm standing in the corner,
crying.

My hands are not my own.
They're trembling.

I wear hand-me-down
t-shirt and trousers.

I'm in a one room house
with a pot-belly stove,
no indoor plumbing.

The bed is unmade.

It is cold, crowded.

It is hard to breathe.

In the Story of My Father

the clothes are all blue and white,
the days begin before first light,
when the dog's howl is still hollow,
when owls hoot and look for field mice.

In the story of my father
a black lunch box opens
to warm cheese sandwiches
and coal black coffee.
The odor of carcasses blinds
and dulls the sense of smell.

It is a black smell
of lifting soaked hides onto hooks
for long Pennsylvania days
in a tannery built next to a creek
where blood trickles from drain pipes
and clots at the neck.

In the story of my father
I am hated more than loved
and feel that I deserve to be pushed down,
I deserve to be forced to kill our pets,
bury them as they die one by one.

In the story of my father
I do not belong to his suffering
except that I am alive
and take food from him.

There is much which is not said
and little that is shown.

There are guns and blood and death
in the eyes of my father.

And there is the story of my father
in the story of me.

War

A bottle of beer, wedged
between Dad's legs
while he drove, unsettled
Mom all the way
to my growing up.

A functioning alcoholic, Dad
had a steady hand
and a slow eye,
World War II
running through his chest.

He could outwork
most men, no matter
the job. His arms, legs,
and back strong,
the tannery kept him on
during large layoffs.

When the tannery left town,
the foundry, the wrecking crew,
and High School found work
for him until the last
of his energy gave way
to the weight of all he'd seen.

Cheating the Deer

Dad built our house along
Beautys Run Road in a hollow
he knew well because
he hunted there for years.

Deer crossed our front porch
late in twilight evenings.

We hunted the hills
anyway, settling into an early
snow like a security blanket,
waiting to get a bead on a buck
as it rushed over a knoll
or traveled slowly through woods
taking footsteps that sounded
human to the untrained ear.

After years of hunting,
the deer sidetracked us,
leaped over the embankment
near our ten acre field
of lost dreams.

Standing near the barn,
we'd shoot them as they flew
through the air and they'd tumble
into a heap of winter dinners.

Food Line

The peanut butter my dad
stood in a long line for
needed to be stirred.
Peanut oil seeped to the top
and tasted like peanuts,
but had the texture of castor oil.
Using a long knife, he stirred
an endless circle in the fat can.

After standing in the food line,
Dad went on job interviews
and waited in other lines
for jobs as janitor, well-driller,
fix-it man. For cigarette and beer money,
our neighbors gave Dad gifts of odd jobs.

At dinner, peanut butter was offered
along with orange cheese and Spam.
Dad waited for the five of us
to select our meal.
Seldom hungry and always thin,
Dad ate what was left over
if there was anything.

Kickball

We played on the lower
recess field where the swings
were and the monkey bars.
Our kickball was not filled
tightly with air and so thudded
into the sky, a mushroom
at the end of the foot.

Behind the outfield
was a short bank,
then the road, the guardrail
and the steep hill
down to the creek
which is where I traveled,
unexcused and against school policy,
after the kickball I had failed
to stop.

My classmates yelled for me
not to go, one screeched
when I just shot
across the road unattended.

Once over the steel thread
of the guardrail, the sound
of running water
and crunching leaves underfoot,
and wind like angel breath
touching the trees.

There was no reason for me
to face the recess monitor
or to return to face my failure.

They had told my parents.
I was "Impossible to handle."

So I waited, sitting on the deflated
ball, for the final bell to ring
and buses to roll up into place.
No one came for me.

I got on the bus with the other kids.
No one talked to the difficult child,
the independent one, and no one called
my home to tell of my temporary
disappearance.

There was no one to tell
that I'd skipped stones, saw fish
travel upstream through rapids,
heard the trucks down on the highway,
felt angel breath on my face
and the soft touch of myself
deep inside me thinking
how important is kickball anyway.

Shooting Puppies

The tiny black and white puppy yelped.
Blood dotted its forehead
as it lay down in the hole
I had dug in the thick dirt
of the back yard, near the telephone pole.

There were seven in all to kill,
but the twenty-two had become heavy,
and my eight-year-old hands shook
just like the final shudder
of the first puppy's body.

One grave for seven little bodies
we could not give away
and could not afford to feed.
Eventually, the grave was filled.
I covered over the hole with the soil
from the same yard we played in.

Saving Lives

In the back
of the old Plymouth,
permanently parked
deep in weeds,
was a nest of field mice,
often called pests
and killed with the heel
of a well worn boot.

The tiny family
of little-finger sized,
pink, eyes closed, squeaking
babies nestled in the stuffing
that leaked from the torn seat.

Not wishing to disturb
their home,
I straightened up the weeds,
erased my sneaker prints,
and sat near the front fender
in the heat of Summer,
listening to tiny sounds
only I could hear.

The Dried Run

Beautys Run dried up each summer
leaving patches of water
for minnows, polliwogs, and crayfish.

Walking up the stone bed
I thought of water
once there, how it would run
over my feet, around
my legs. I thought of suckers
that spawned in spring,
of hard ice we skated over
wearing only shoes.

I saw the run
from a new angle,
from the fish or frog
point of view.

Branches reached down
to touch where water
might have been, roots protruded
from banks. Rabbit dens grew dry.
Snakes came down from the dry
mountain, into the valley,
and along the stream beds
that paralleled the road
all the way up to the church.

Wife Abuse

At 2 a.m. we heard the screams
coming from somewhere in the valley.
High pitched harpies
rising toward the moon
caught in pine trees
but a hurricane wind
tore them loose to slap the macadam
and roll up Beautys Run Road.

We kids got dressed
and drove down the road with Dad.
"Probably Carl's beating his wife again,"
he told us.
It was the first I'd heard
of such a thing, the sound on the air
made more sorrowful by his words.
Chills moved up my back
and across my shoulders.
I wished I could no longer hear at all.

But we passed Carl's and the lights
were out, the car missing.
Farther down the road we saw
the Shaw boys squealing and whooping.
We stopped and Dad got out to talk.

It was all very pleasant and civilized.
They even said thank you and waved
goodbye as we left.
They stopped their painful howling.

That night, sleep was difficult
to regain. I took a long walk
up the run bank early
in the still-wet morning.
The trees leaned
with the sound of something
that had never happened.

Carl had been in the hospital
that morning: a heart attack.
How difficult it was to feel bad
for the man I'd always liked,
who seemed to like me,
with that sound, that horrible,
clutching, begging, shameful sound
brought in his name
falsely to my ears.

The Big Rock

I loved sitting
on the solid rock
kept cool by the flowing water
of Beautys Run.

A deep hole
on one side held suckers in tight reflections.
They waited for bugs
or fishing lines and worms.

It was my island far away from the familiar
ground of our backyard.
When alone, I'd meditate
on the world of comics and super heroes.

When anyone yelled for me,
I pretended that the run was a river,
that the rock was Tom Sawyer's raft,
that I was too far down stream to be called home.

Home

Summers, Dad was always looking
for work. He refused to move
with the company he repaired
looms for. Then the tannery shut down.

Winters got progressively colder
at our house. Neighbors could be only so generous.
Mom's face was that of an optimist,
but she had a pessimist between her ears.

Dad never finished the home he built for us—
no siding, half a porch, yard of weeds,
a creekbed that overflowed each spring.

Those days, I was up at five, outside shoveling dirt
around, trying to create a driveway that wouldn't
fill with mud, leveling the front yard, getting ready
for my future in the labor force.

Pointing the Barrel

There he stood
next to a tree,
rifle in hand,
hanging loosely
near his right thigh.

And there I stood
somewhere, years maybe,
to the right of him, pointing
my 44-40 at his blond head.
He was the younger brother,
the pampered one,
always sick, always protected.

He went to college prep,
while I was forced,
like a key through a keyhole,
to go to technical school.
No money for college, forced
to get a job quickly
and start contributing.

One pull of the trigger
and it would have been
all over for both of us.

The Black Man

It might have been against
those delicate social rules
explained to me later in life,
but the black man standing
with Dad on our front porch
holding a beer we had given him
was a friend of the family.

My mom hugged him and Dad
held his shoulder like a son.
They laughed together and swore
and laughed together again.
I liked him better than Dad's other
friend who always called us kids shits.
This man was hard-working
Dad said and kind enough
that children knew it.

He owned his own blacktopping
business, but could hardly find any
whites to hire him. He lived poor
and scraping. He gave us my favorite
German Shepherd dog
out of friendship. I learned later
he was not allowed into
certain restaurants downtown
or the bars my dad went to.

The black man was found
beaten to death in an alley,

four hundred dollars in his wallet.
Mom cried all night.
Dad paced the floor and swore.
If his friend had been there
he could have made them laugh.

Hay Ride

Drops of fire-slobber
drift through the air
on parachutes of wind.

Teenage children, look up
toward an unknown light, hold hands.
There's a fire on Kinley's farm.

Here a wagon filled with hay
and teenagers will ride through
the cold woods.
The kids will clutch onto
the warmth of one another's bodies.

It will be a night of first feels,
bulging crotches, hands searching for
what they believe
is the sole answer to their futures.

The Tree House

She had breasts you couldn't
keep off your mind.

We were two virgins.
I'd grown up in woods:
my whole life tree bark,
rotting leaves, branches
and a tree house made
from useless wood.

Late night, an all day tiredness
hanging over us, brought her within reach.
The moon wasn't the only thing up.
Voices never sounded so good:
hers so close and feminine, so sure.
I was shaking worse than Jell-O.

Thank the moon for being high.
Thank the tree house for being high.

This is the reason I live on,
why the moon is my favorite celestial
body, why in my eyes, the trees always
hold themselves so strong and sure.

Headless

At ten, I rode my bike up the road
away from home and found upon
my return a seven foot
black snake stretched
across the macadam.

Dad ran outside
when I hollered, grabbed
a garden hoe on his way.

Even headless that snake
twitched all afternoon,
looking for something
it didn't have. Dad said,
"It'll do that until sundown."

But, without a head,
I wondered how it would know.

After the killing, Dad left
and I sat nearby.
The snake coiled
around the stick of my arm
as though complaining
about its misfortune,
something I understood.

That night, I worried
our black sentinel was gone
forever. I dreamed of being headless,
waiting for the final flicker of sun.

Beyond Death

Near the burned grass
of the side field,
in a branch and twig filled
bend in the winding run,
the remains of a deer spread
out in foam and sinew.

Its head twisted back
near relocated hoof and leg bone,
its body leaned like a hollow
brown sack into the flowing water.

With each ripple and gluck,
more of the deer tore loose
to be carried in the direction
of the Susquehanna River,
somewhere beyond Lycoming Creek,
somewhere beyond death.

Return to the Earth

In the house of my childhood
I saw through the floorboard cracks
into the dirt basement.
The toilet, a deep hole dug
under a skinny shed, sat
to the right of the back steps.

During long nights under heavy blankets
I wet my bed rather than brave
the dark hall to the tin bucket waiting
in the dark closet-sized room
that was supposed to be a bathroom.

The bedroom windows let in
so much cold,
frost lined the windowsill,
and part of the wall.
I could smell winter
and part of me wanted to be
part of the outside world
covered in warm blankets of snow.

In spring I cleared weeds
from the yard where I found
a hammer and hoe almost planted,
stuck amid the colors of rust, grass,
and dirt. The tools lay as though
they too wanted to return to the Earth.

The Butternut Tree

As I climbed
the trunk of the butternut tree,
all arms and legs
wrapped around it,
Dad drove me onward,
to chase a butterfly I never saw.

Sun seeped through clouds throwing
patches of shadow over the ground.
I climbed beyond my fear of heights
and beyond dangerous.

Today, I wonder if Dad was proving
to the visiting uncle
my climbing ability or the strength
of his control over my actions?

I remember taking advantage
of what I wasn't allowed to do,
pushing past the first branches.

And while Dad sat on the ground
watching me, I never realized
that I'd keep pushing,
that eventually he'd come to
resent the fearlessness he taught me.

II

Dad

There was a slant
to the sun
the day you beat me
because I disobeyed
the lock and key
of a statement, an order
I swear you never said.

I cried the sap tears
of a pine branch
then ran, head first,
into the wall of marriage.

When you died,
I felt beaten again,
only your fists
had turned to leaves
as they fell into my hands.

I didn't cry
as I remembered
what you never
had to say.

Bottle Cap

Shining
in the back
of the crawl space,
under the half-finished
porch still bare except
for floorboards torn
from the old barn up the road,
the one that stood there thirty
years or more before falling in
on its own, was an old bottle cap
from a long-drunk beer my father
probably nursed after working long hours
at the tannery downtown near the creek.
Its reflection of what little light
there was under the house reminded
me of how his eyes gleamed brightly
only just before he fell
asleep on the old chair that still sits,
like a dead leper, alone
in the living room of the old
house where he lived almost
his entire life without
ever really talking
to me.

Conversation

Do you ever wonder
what the world is telling you?
The trees as they bend,
the mountain formations
from ten thousand feet up?

Why do the robins, hundreds
of them, fly into the bush
right next to where
you are standing?

What is being said?

Do you ever think to respond?

The Back Roads

For a few years, Dad
drove a well-drilling rig
where he and a buddy, whose
daughter I crushed on,
stood around and watched to make
sure nothing went wrong.

All that standing around
and a war incident—
where my dad was forced to lie
in cold water for hours, nothing
but his nose in the air—resulted
in him always having cold feet,
which he passed on to me.

Whenever I was around a girl
of intimidating wealth or beauty
my feet became glaciers.
I never said anything to the daughter
unless she asked, and Dad never
complained about the cold.

We stole only a few minutes
of warmth our whole lives,
him in a heated cab and
me in a warm bed, no matter
whose it was.

Fly Home

How many times have I eaten
breakfast alone
and in a hotel room
overlooking a cityscape—
mostly rooftops, sides
of buildings emptying
into canyons of streets
and people going,

always going but never arriving?

In the distance,
the train never stops
running in circles
around the Christmas
Tree of New York.
The train's rumble
is reminiscent of hunger
that can't be allayed.

I let go of my song,
my famished song,
into the air outside
the eighth story window.

May it fly.

And Now This

Divorces, several, and before
thirty-five, as though not man
enough to keep a woman
satisfied for more than a few
years.

My work suffered while
going through all that confusion.
Children added to the mix,
I found that foundation my life
was pouring had fallen before
being completely erected–
poetry the sawdust.

I lived in half the eastern seaboard
states while finding a place to be
comfortable with my self,
some nuance of peace.

Cancer reminded me this house
wasn't about to be saved
so easily, and now this: the poetry
sounds mundane,
whistling along the blank page,
while my roof is full of leaks.

Fed

Took the boys on that Ohio
Steam Train attraction hoping
there'd be history covered
during the lecture portion.
Being of American Indian heritage
on my father's side,

I couldn't predict
my boys would connect with
the burial mounds representing
ancestors they didn't know.

Maybe callused at my age,
those grassy knolls rose
in the past somewhere, a time
I never lived, a time outside
my emotional understanding.

But for my boys there were people
under that ground, who couldn't breathe,
couldn't move, or see, scattered
like stones over a riverbed.

To them our ancestors were tortured,
held down by the same people
who they fed,
who they taught how to farm
when it was needed most.

Friend

The shuffle of bird wings
and scrape of clouds across the velcro
tops of mountains disturbs me.
The taut violin-string air
has me on edge.

Then comes the call
about your death.
The phone vanishes
from my hand.

I am transported to a day
we sat cross-legged in the hay loft,
your pale hands opening
the stolen magazine to photos
of naked women.
You asked me which one I liked best.

Progress

They fixed
the highway
near Old Oak Road.

Now when you reach
the ridge
on Bastion's Hill

you can't see
the old oak.

Under the Surface

Airmen, too, know the fine line
between sky and ground, and how
easy it is to get lost between.

One time a young pilot lost control
and crashed an F-4 Phantom
I had repaired the night before. My loss
of sleep couldn't change that.

Every mistake is attributed
to pilot error. Ground crews know
better. They glance at each other
during breaks, double-check fuel lines,
hydraulics cables, electronics equipment
like the altimeter I repaired,
which is more complex than most
technicians understand.

In a dream I couldn't control how close
to the ground I flew.
I had forgotten
which direction was up.

The Stock Barn Fire

Ours was a broken down
well-used Chevy truck, so rusty
the emblems fell off years before.
That was my dating ride, good
for about one date. No girl
wanted to be seen with me more
than once, but when I did
find one I got her pregnant.

One night, long before marriage
I drove toward home past
the stock barn.
It was burning bright,
the flames eating up loose hay
and Pennsylvania Pine.

I was too young to be out past
midnight, with police everywhere,
with all those animal souls screaming
about the things I'd already done wrong.

Cemetary Dance

Those long walks at 3 a.m.
after we fought, after we cried,
always took me to the cemetery
and I don't know why.

One thing found its way
into my blue heart
on those sandpaper nights,
an acceptance of death perhaps,
or a tolerance for hostility, maybe
a crow's understanding that there are
two worlds and that I don't have to live
in one alone.

The flame defused,
I'd walk home a deprived,
but tamed man of the night.

Even into old age,
I've brought the peace of darkness
with me, the eloquence of letting go
of the hard stone of another's heart.

Blank Slate

One date, really.
Parked at the lake, no shirt,
no bra. You said, "How much
more vulnerable could I be?
What more do you want?"

We kissed, and played
that game we all love
and hate. You were Gail,
and I was stormed over.

We went to the adult movie,
watched others do what
we wanted. Watched.
Nothing more.

Shadows darkened
the time we spent together,
our hearts hopeful but harnessed
to other hearts.

What did we think would happen?
We tempted every way we could.

Mourning

I watch my workaholic life
play out like a long rope
on the time spool. The mortgage
hounds me like a junk yard
dog hounds an old alley cat.

Can't live a single month
without telephones and Internet,
shelter and a warm cup of soup.
I've gotten myself so used
to nightlights I'm afraid
of the dark, even when moonlight
buckles through the closed shades.

And all this time, I stand by
and watch what I love to do
sift through misty air
like wannabe clouds hanging
over to the river,
which already found
a way out of town.

Love Poem

Who else would help empty
the catheter bag but you,
blame me for working
too hard, for depleting
the bank accounts
of my heart just to hear
you breathe next to me?

Eyes can't lie or shaking
hands, when you reach
for my face while
making love.

This ride,
this body, this soul
has paid its dues.

There is nothing left
but age and memory.

Nothing left
but the sweet taste
of us

as day dims
into the borders
of night.

Notes

She often wrote notes
to herself, reminders to pick
up bread or cereal, warnings
not to go up Ballard Street
because the guard dog jogged,
unleashed, behind a flimsy
picket fence; notes that told
stories—Donna took too many
pills again, but only slept
for a few days—about friends
or acquaintances; and decisions
concerning taking a class
or joining a friend for coffee.

So when I folded back
the checkbook
she used to pay our bills,
and a card dropped to the desktop
making a sharp sound,
my first reaction was not to read it,
to let it disappear like her last
breath before she left
this world over a month ago.
But I glanced and saw
my name and couldn't help
but read what she had planned
for my birthday,

which I had completely forgotten
was the day
she said her last I love you.

Writing Poetry

I shuffle back and forth
to the kitchen whenever
I want coffee. No one
lives with me anymore,
they've all left or died.

When I look back
into the room where I sit
with my desk lamp
and computer and paper,
it looks as though everything
is inside a dark tunnel
with a slight glow
from a single bulb.

How many years, I wonder,
have I sat at that desk
and written or rewritten
not knowing who might
or might not read my words,
who might or might not
care about what my thoughts
focused on or landed near?

I scratch my rough beard
of three days, and pour
another cup of coffee
before I wander back
into that dark tunnel
to listen, to smell, to feel
what else is inside me,
scrambling to get out.

My Sister's Heart Attack

Ponies live a long time
if cared for, and Nosey
got brushed daily, fed
grain and clean hay
for all the years my sister
lived at home.

Marriage stole her away,
but Nosey stayed
and became too much for Mom.

Nosey lived on though, pastured
in a side field that flooded
once a year, overflowing the old
tires we stuffed rocks into
to make a water barrier.

Nosey grazed through my sister's
divorce, the birth of a daughter, death
of a husband, until she foundered,
struggled, and lay down in high grass
for good.

Nosey, mourned and remembered,
rides through woods, the agreeable hills,
and dry summer creek beds,
like a long breath
drawing near the end.

The Question Never Asked

Dad told me years later,
"I always hated you." Old
photos indicate my dark skin,
where my brothers and sister
showed white.

Pennsylvania Dutch, German,
even Italian kids called me
nigger until I climbed the fence,
ran off the playground.

When asked which picture
on our family wall of photos
was me, Dad would say,
"He's the black one."

What I didn't know and still don't
was if he thought his best friend
had anything to do
with my skin color.

Dad stayed with Mom, I suspect
not knowing.
Yet, as years passed
I looked more like Dad
than when I was a child.

Now the mirror answers
the question,
but Dad will never
hear it from the grave.

Staring into the Past

A two-foot snow and icy rains gripped
the town while we delivered major
appliances to farms in the county.
Our Econoline Van dragged its cargo
along increasingly unsympathetic roads,
the heater struggling worse than the tires
to hold onto a semblance of dignity.

The white day hummed like a train
receding into a moist fog, like the woods
at night, like a frightening sorrow
that attacks the eyes, wringing out tears.

The freight delivered and cozy
in its new home, the van lightened
like an empty heart. We thought
going home would be easy.

Mid-afternoon traffic squirmed
over icy roads down the slope
of the last legs of our journey when
the van spun around and
sped backward down the hill,
still heading home as we
stared into the space we had just been.

Only packed snow on the median
stayed our demise.

On Leaving

I stand in the middle
of the hay field
as it leans one way,
and on a windless morning
shifts miraculously,
like a school of fish,
in a new direction.

The tall grass and I live
among invisible winds—
or some other miracle—
that leans against me until
the fish carry my heart
in a new direction.

At the closing of day,
the sun brightens everything
it touches,
and it touches me.

Backlit as though I am
a holy man, I extend
my arms to accept the dusk,
golden light
spreading out as far
as I can see,

golden light drawing the best
out of everything it touches,
everything it can't touch.

About the Author

Terry Persun is a full-time writer, and has published two poetry collections, six poetry chapbooks, and seven novels through small, independent presses. His latest novel, *Cathedral of Dreams*, was a finalist for the ForeWord magazine Book of the Year Award, and his literary novel, *Sweet Song*, won a Silver IPPY Award.

Terry's poems and short stories have been published in numerous independent and university journals, including *Wisconsin Review, Yarrow, Riverrun, NEBO, Oyez Review, Hiram Poetry Review, Owen Wister Review, Kansas Quarterly, Rag Mag, Poet Lore, Whiskey Island, Colorado-North Review, Widener Review, Context South* and many others.

Other Poetry Collections by Terry Persun

Books
Every Leaf, published by March Street Press
Barn Tarot, published by Implosion Press

Chapbooks
In the Story, published by Implosion Press
Three Lives, published by Proper pH
Plant-Animal-I, published by March Street Press
Hollow Goodbyes, published by mulberry press
Dandelion Soul, published by Nightshade Press
Behind a Red Gate, published by Implosion Press

www.ingramcontent.com/pod-product-compliance
Lightning Source LLC
Chambersburg PA
CBHW032005060426
42449CB00031B/614